My First Book of Card Tricks

Written by Gordon Hill
Photography by Nigel Goldsmith

p

Contents

Introduction

Doing card tricks is great fun. There are lots of tricks in this book for you to learn.

Try them out in private first. When you can do a trick really well you can show it to your friends. They will be amazed at your magical skills but do not tell them how the tricks are done. When people know how the tricks are done they will not enjoy them so much.

Have fun with your card tricks!

Flying Ace

A card vanishes from the pack and flies invisibly to a place you decide upon.

You will need:
• a pack of cards

Secret preparation

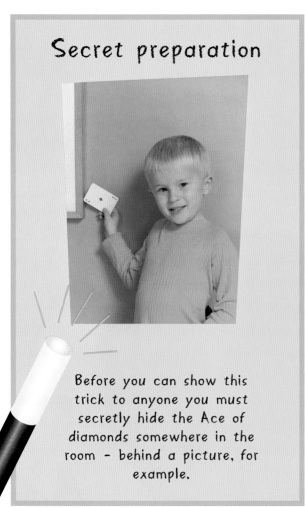

Before you can show this trick to anyone you must secretly hide the Ace of diamonds somewhere in the room - behind a picture, for example.

1 Take the Ace of spades, the Ace of clubs and the Ace of hearts from the pack. Do not let anyone see what cards you have taken.

Place the Ace of hearts behind the other two Aces so that only the bottom part of the big heart can be seen.

2

3 Show the cards to the audience and say: "Ace of spades, Ace of diamonds and Ace of clubs". As the Ace of hearts looks like a diamond the audience will believe this.

Place the three cards on top of the pack and then put them, one at a time, into different parts of the pack as you say: "Ace of diamonds, Ace of clubs and the Ace of spades."

4

5

Pretend to take an invisible card from the pack as you say: "I have made the Ace of diamonds invisible and am now taking it from the pack."

6 Ask someone to go through the pack to make certain that the Ace of diamonds has indeed disappeared.

7 Now say that you are going to make the invisible Ace of diamonds travel through the air and behind a picture.

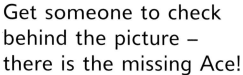

8

Get someone to check behind the picture – there is the missing Ace!

Cards Across

An Ace of spades is put into one box and an Ace of diamonds is put into another. Magically, the two cards change places!

You will need:
- 2 boxes
- 2 special cards

Secret preparation

1 To make the special cards you need two Aces of spades, two Aces of diamonds and some glue.

2 Glue each Ace of diamonds back to back with each Ace of spades.

3 You now have two cards with the Ace of diamonds on one side and the Ace of spades on the other.

1 Show the two empty boxes.

2 Show one card with the Ace of spades showing and the other with the Ace of diamonds side facing the audience.

3

Put the Ace of spades in the box on your left and the Ace of diamonds in the box on the right. Be careful not to show the other side of the cards as you do this.

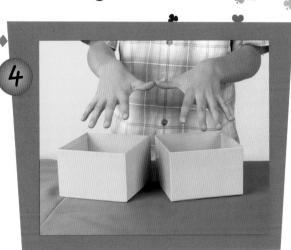

4

Wave your hands over the two boxes in a mysterious manner.

5

Put a hand into the left box, secretly turning the card around as you take it out to show the audience - it is the Ace of diamonds.

6

Go the other box and bring out the other card, again secretly turning it around so the Ace of spades is now seen by the audience.

7

Your magic powers have made the two Aces change places.

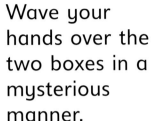

Ever-changing Card

You show the audience a large card – it appears to be the Ace of diamonds – or is it?

You will need:
• a special card (approx 15cm x 20cm)

How to make it

1 For the special card you will need a piece of white card and a red pen.

2 Use the red pen to draw two diamonds on one side of the card and five diamonds on the other side. The pictures show how the diamonds must be positioned.

1 Hold the card in your right hand with the two of diamonds side facing the audience but with your hand covering the bottom diamond. Everyone will think you are holding an Ace of diamonds. Say "One".

8

2 Place your left hand over the diamond in the centre of the back of the card.

Turn the left hand, and the card, over to show a four of diamonds. Your fingers cover the diamond in the centre of the card. Say "Four".

4 Now place your right hand over the space below the two diamonds on the other side of the card.

5

The right hand now turns the card over to show what appears to be three diamonds (with your hand apparently covering the third diamond). Say "Three".

6 Now cover the space in the centre of the back of the card with your right hand.

7 Turn the card over and say "Six". With practice you will be able to position your hands and turn the card over quickly.

9

Clipped Cards

A paper clip is placed over one card within a group, but when the cards are turned over the paper clip is not where it appears to be!

You will need:
- a special card
- a paper clip

How to make it

Glue five playing cards together, overlapping the cards as in the picture so that each card is visible. Make sure there is a prominent card, such as the Queen of clubs, in the centre of the group.

1 Show the five glued cards.

2

Point to the Queen of clubs in the middle of the group.

3 Turn the cards face down.

4

Hand out the paper clip and ask someone to put it on the Queen of clubs.

Slowly turn the cards over. Everyone will be surprised to see that the clip is on a card at the end of the group, quite a distance from the Queen of clubs!

5

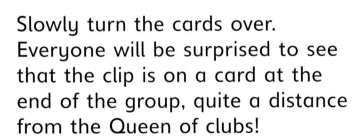

Magic Match

You remove two cards from a shuffled pack. A spectator cuts the cards and the cards cut to exactly match the ones you selected earlier.

You will need:
- a pack of cards

1 Ask someone to shuffle the cards to make sure they are well mixed.

2 Take the cards back and say you are going to take out two cards. Without letting anyone know what cards you are taking, go through the pack and take out the card that most closely matches the card on the bottom of the pack (if the bottom card is the six of diamonds, for example, you take out the six of hearts).

3

Place the card you have taken, face down, on the table, then go through the pack again.

4

This time take out the card that matches the card at the top of the pack. Then place it, face down, on the table.

5 Place the pack down on the table.

6 Ask someone to lift off a portion of the pack and place it to one side on the table.

7 The rest of the pack is then put down on top of the cut-off portion but at a 90° angle to it.

8 Remind the spectators of what has happened - the pack was shuffled by one of the audience and someone else cut the cards at a random point.

9 Say: "Let's see what cards you cut to" as you lift up the top portion of the pack and show the bottom card, then show the top card of the lower portion.

10 Now turn over the two cards you took earlier – they match the chosen cards!

The Detectives

Three Aces are used to find the fourth Ace that is lost somewhere in the pack.

You will need:
* a pack of cards

Secret preparation:

1 Take out the four Aces and put them on top of the pack.

2 Lift off the top three Aces and hide one card on top of the second Ace.

Show the three Aces (be careful not to let anyone see the hidden card).

1

2 Say that the fourth Ace has gone missing in the wild wood and that the pack of cards will represent the wild wood.

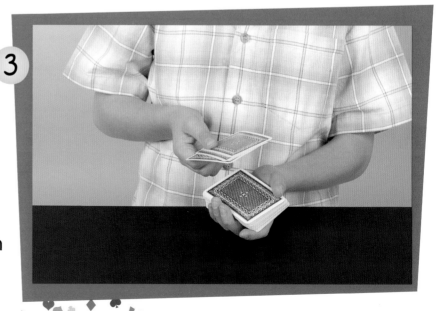

3

Say that the other three Aces have decided to go into the wild wood to find their friend. Place the Aces (and the hidden card) on top of the pack.

"The first Ace decided to go to the far side of the wood in case his friend came out on that side." As you say this take the top card (an Ace) and place it on the bottom of the pack.

Take the next card from the top of the pack (do not let anyone see it as it is not an Ace) and push it into the centre of the pack as you say, "The second Ace decided to search in the middle of the wood."

Leave the 'third' Ace on top of the pack as you say, "The third Ace stayed on this side of the wood in case his friend came out on this side."

Cut the pack, putting the bottom half onto the top and say, "The three Aces had agreed that if their friend was not found they should all meet in the centre of the wood."

Turn the cards face up and spread them out to show the four Aces all together in the centre of the pack. Say: "When they reached the centre of the wild wood they were relieved to find that their friend was already there!"

Quick Change

You show your audience a King of hearts. As you pass your hand over it the card changes to the Ace of spades!

How to make it

1 To make the special card you will need some glue and three playing cards – a King of hearts, an Ace of spades and one other card.

2 Fold the King and the Ace in half.

3 Now glue the two folded cards to each other and to the face of the third card, as shown.

4 You now have a card that shows the King of hearts when the central flap is held against the top of the rear card and the Ace of spades when the flap is downwards.

1

Hold the card in your left hand with the flap upwards so the King of hearts is facing the audience.

Bring your right hand up to cover the top part of the King.

2

3 Move your right hand downward pushing the flap down at the same time. Hold your right hand out flat when doing this so it hides the movement of the flap.

4 When the flap has moved all the way down take your right hand away and everyone will see that the card has changed to and Ace.

17

Magnetic Cards

You place several cards on your hand and then turn your hand over. The audience expects them to fall to the floor but they remain clinging to your hand by some magnetic magic.

You will need:
- a few playing cards
- a special card

How to make it

1 Cut a small piece from the centre of an old playing card with the same back design as the rest of the cards you are going to use.

2 Fold the small piece of card in half and glue one half of it to the back of another card.

3 You now have a tab on the back of the card that lays flat against the card until you need it.

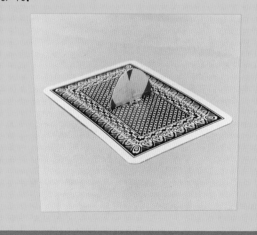

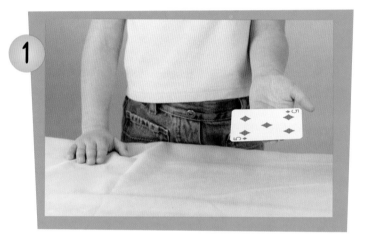

1 Pick up the special card and put it face up on the palm of your left hand.

2 Move the card until you can open the tab and hold it between two of your fingers.

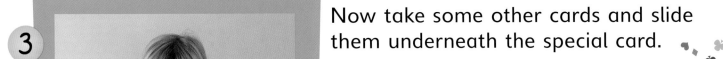

3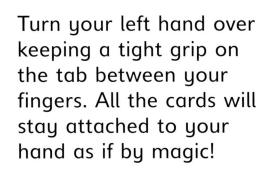

Now take some other cards and slide them underneath the special card.

Turn your left hand over keeping a tight grip on the tab between your fingers. All the cards will stay attached to your hand as if by magic!

4

After the audience has applauded this amazing feat look intently at your left hand and shout "Go" as you let go of the tab. All the cards will fall onto your table.

5

6 As you gather up the cards hide the special card among the others so there is no clue as to how the trick was done.

All in the Mind

You read a spectator's mind to name a chosen card without seeing the cards.

You will need:
• a pack of cards

1 Ask a spectator to shuffle the cards and then take out any card but not a picture card (in other words – not a Jack, Queen or King).

2 The spectator then shows the card to everyone else before placing it, face down, on top of the pack.

3 Now ask the spectator to take a number of cards from the bottom of the pack to match the value of the chosen card (if the chosen card is a seven, for example, seven cards will be taken from the bottom of the pack).

4 The removed cards should now be placed on the top of the pack.

Now ask the spectator to deal cards, one at a time, from the top of the pack onto the table calling out the name of each card as it is dealt. The spectator must keep dealing right past the chosen card until you call out "Stop".

5

6 You then name the chosen card.

7

As the spectator calls out the names of the cards you ignore the first one and then count silently to yourself. When the spectator calls out a card that corresponds to the number you have counted to that is the chosen card.

A point to remember: Sometimes there will be more than one card matching your silent count. If this is the case you will have to guess which is the chosen card. If you guess wrong, immediately name the other card.

Card Control

Five red cards and five black cards are mixed together, some face up and some face down. You hold the cards behind your back, divide them in half and the number of face up and face down cards in each half is exactly the same.

1

You will need:
• a pack of cards

Take five red cards and five black cards from the pack.

2 Put the two groups face to face – in other words all the cards of one colour are face upwards and the other colour are face downwards.

3

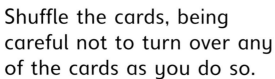

Shuffle the cards, being careful not to turn over any of the cards as you do so.

4

Take the cards behind your back and count off the top five cards. Turn these cards over in your hand.

6

5 Bring both groups of cards forward and spread them in two separate groups on the table.

Each group will have the same number of face up cards. Not only that but the face up cards in each group will all be of the same colour!

7 You can do this trick again if you wish but be careful to turn over one of the groups before you put all the cards together again.

Future Sight

A card is chosen by a spectator. Another person opens an envelope, handed out earlier, inside which is a piece of paper naming the chosen card - written before the performance!

1 Hand the sealed envelope to someone and ask them to keep it safe for the time being.

Secret preparation

1 Before showing this trick take a look at the ninth card from the top of the pack and then put the pack back in its box.

2 Write the name of the card you saw at the ninth position on the slip of paper, put the paper into the envelope and seal it.

24

2 Remove the pack of cards from its box and ask someone else to call out any number between 10 and 20.

Count off that number of cards from the top of the pack and onto the table.

4 Pick up the cards you have just dealt as you point out that the chosen number (between 10 and 20) consists of two digits.

5 Add the two digits together and count off that number of cards from the top of the cards you are holding. If, for example, 17 was the chosen number you would count off eight cards (1 + 7), if 13 was chosen then count off four cards (1 + 3).

6

Show everyone the next card on the top of the cards you are holding (this will be the card you saw at the ninth position earlier).

Ask the person with the envelope to open it and read out what you wrote before the show. It is the name of the selected card!

7

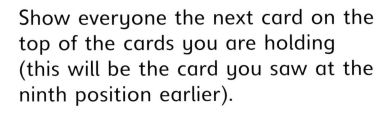

Your Card

A card is chosen and returned to the pack before a spectator magically guides your hand to the selected card.

1 Ask a spectator to shuffle the cards.

Take the cards back and spread them face up to show that they are well mixed. What you are really doing is looking at the bottom card. You must remember this card.

2

3

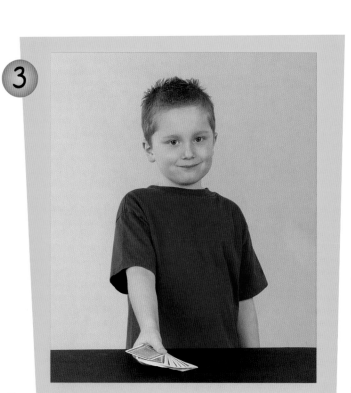

Turn the pack back face down and spread them out as you ask someone to take any card, show it to the audience and remember it.

Ask the spectator to put the card, face down, on top of the pack.

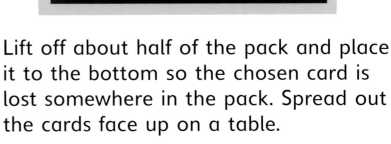

Lift off about half of the pack and place it to the bottom so the chosen card is lost somewhere in the pack. Spread out the cards face up on a table.

Get someone to hold your wrist as you pass your hand over the cards. You can say that this helps you to pick up the vibrations of the chosen card.

While moving your hand over the pack, look for the card you saw on the bottom at the start of the trick. The card to the right of your card is the card the spectator chose.

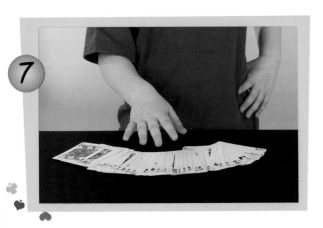

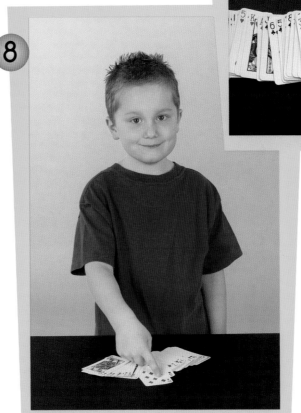

Suddenly bring your hand down and pick out the chosen card much to everyone's amazement.

With special thanks to our models Daniel Broom, Ida Joof, Michael King, Lucy Down and Daniel Richards.

This is a Parragon book
This edition published 2006

Parragon
Queen Street House
4 Queen Street
Bath BA1 1HE, UK

ISBN 1-40544-740-0
Printed in China